W9-CCA-847

ITALIAN COOKING

JG PRESS

2061
Published in the USA 1995 by JG Press
Distributed by World Publications, Inc
Copyright © 1994 by Colour Library Books Ltd ,Godalming, Surrey
All rights reserved
No part of this book may be reproduced or transmitted in any
form or by any means, electronic or mechanical, including
photocopying, recording, or by any information storage and
retrieval system, without permission in writing from the Publisher.
Printed and Bound in Singapore
ISBN 1-57215-017-3

The JG Press imprint is a trademark of JG Press, Inc.
455 Somerset Avenue
North Dighton, MA 02764

INTRODUCTION

The food of Italy is among the best-loved in the world. The ingredients reflect all the warmth, color and variety that the country has to offer. There are beautiful lemons, limes and oranges in the orchards up and down the peninsula. Miles and miles of coastline mean a plentiful supply of fish and seafood. Tomatoes, peppers and most other vegetables flourish in the sun throughout spring and summer. Herbs, garlic and the fragrant bouquet of olive oil all provide taste interest. Cheeses and cured meats are superb in quality and selection.

When putting together a traditional Italian meal, begin with an antipasto, which means "before the pasta." Follow with a pasta dish or soup, but not both. Then choose a main course of fish, meat or poultry accompanied by polenta, risotto or potatoes and a salad. A sweet is served next, and this can be as rich as Zuppa Inglese or as simple as fresh fruit. Cheese is considered an antipasto and not the final course.

Vegetables are highly prized in Italy and often appear as a separate course before the main dish. Sicilian Caponata is a perfect choice, hot or cold.

If all that food seems too much, turn to Italy's best-known contributions, pizza and pasta. Once you make your own pizza dough, you won't go back to frozen pizzas again! Home-made pasta is also a wonderful thing and easy to make, too, but if you can't find time, try to buy fresh pasta, which is readily available these days.

There is room for endless creativity with sauces for pastas and toppings for pizzas so boredom need never set in. Just add a salad and perhaps a glorious pudding like cassata for an authentic taste of Italy that is as close as your kitchen.

SERVES 6-8

BRUSCHETTA WITH TOMATOES

Cooked over a wood fire in the traditional way, or more
conveniently in the oven, tomatoes, basil and crisp bread
make an unusual and informal appetizer.

18 slices of crusty Italian bread, cut 1 inch thick
2 cloves garlic, crushed
½ cup olive oil
Salt and pepper
18 large fresh basil leaves
4-5 ripe tomatoes, depending on size

Step 1 Toast the bread in the oven until golden brown on both sides and spread each side with some of the garlic.

1. Place the bread slices on a baking sheet and toast for about 10 minutes on each side at 375°F.

2. Spread some of the garlic on both sides of each slice.

3. Heat the oil gently in a small saucepan. Arrange the bread on a serving plate and immediately pour over the warm oil. Sprinkle with salt and pepper.

Step 3 Warm the oil in a small saucepan and pour over the bread.

Step 4 Slice the tomatoes with a serrated knife and arrange on top of the bread with the basil leaves.

4. Slice the tomatoes in ½ inch rounds. Place one basil leaf and one slice of tomato on each slice of bread and serve immediately.

Cook's Notes

Time
Preparation takes about 15 minutes, cooking time about 25 minutes.

Variations
French bread may be used if Italian bread is not available, but the taste will be different. White or brown bread may be used.

Serving Ideas
May be served as a first course or as cocktail savories.

SERVES 4

MELON AND PROSCIUTTO

This is one of the best-loved Italian appetizers. It deserves
to be, because the flavor of a ripe melon and the richness
of Italian ham complement one another perfectly.

1 large ripe melon
16 thin slices prosciutto ham

Step 1 Cut the melon in half and scoop out the seeds.

Step 2 Cut the melon in quarters and carefully remove the rind. Cut into thin slices.

Step 3 Roll up the melon in the prosciutto to serve.

1. Cut the melon in half lengthwise, scoop out the seeds and discard them.

2. Cut the melon into quarters and carefully pare off the rind. Cut each quarter into four slices.

3. Wrap each slice of melon in a slice of prosciutto and place on a serving dish. Alternatively, place the melon slices on the dish and cover with the slices of prosciutto, leaving the ends of the melon showing. Serve immediately.

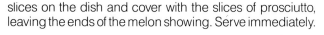

Cook's Notes

Time
Preparation takes about 20 minutes.

Variations
Place the slices of prosciutto flat on serving plates or roll them up into cigar shapes. Serve with quartered fresh figs instead of melon.

SERVES 6-8

SEAFOOD TORTA

A very stylish version of a fish flan, this makes
a perfect accompaniment to an Italian aperitif or
serves as a light supper dish with salad.

Pastry

2 cups all-purpose flour, sifted
½ cup unsalted butter
Pinch salt
4 tbsps cold milk

Filling

4oz whitefish fillets (plaice, sole or cod)
8oz cooked shrimp
4oz flaked crab meat
½ cup white wine
½ cup water
Large pinch hot pepper flakes
Salt and pepper
2 tbsps butter
2 tbsps flour
1 clove garlic, crushed
2 egg yolks
½ cup heavy cream
Chopped fresh parsley

1. To prepare the pastry, sift the flour into a bowl or onto a work surface. Cut the butter into small pieces and begin mixing them into the flour. Mix until the mixture resembles fine breadcrumbs – this may also be done in a food processor. Make a well in the flour, pour in the milk and add the pinch of salt. Mix with a fork, gradually incorporating the butter and flour mixture from the sides until all the ingredients are mixed. This may also be done in a food processor.

2. Form the dough into a ball and knead for about 1 minute. Leave the dough in the refrigerator for about 1 hour.

3. To prepare the filling, cook whitefish fillets in the water and wine with the red pepper flakes for about 10 minutes or

Step 5 Press a sheet of wax paper on the pastry and fill with beans, rice or baking beans to weight down.

until just firm to the touch. When the fish is cooked, remove it from the liquid and flake it into a bowl with the shrimp and the crab meat. Reserve the cooking liquid.

4. Melt the butter in a small saucepan and stir in the flour. Gradually strain on the cooking liquid from the fish, stirring constantly until smooth. Add garlic, place over high heat and bring to the boil. Lower the heat and allow to cook for 1 minute. Add to the fish in the bowl and set aside to cool.

5. On a well-floured surface, roll out the pastry and transfer it with a rolling pin to a tart pan with a removable base. Press the dough into the pan and cut off any excess. Prick the pastry base lightly with a fork and place a sheet of wax paper inside. Fill with rice, dried beans or baking beans and chill for 30 minutes. Bake the pastry shell blind for 15 minutes in a 375°F oven.

6. While the pastry is baking, combine the egg yolks, cream and parsley and stir into the fish filling. Adjust the seasoning with salt and pepper. When the pastry is ready, remove the paper and beans and pour in the filling.

7. Return the tart to the oven and bake for a further 25 minutes. Allow to cool slightly and then remove from the pan. Transfer to a serving dish and slice before serving.

Cook's Notes

Time
Filling takes about 15-20 minutes to prepare. Pastry takes about 20 minutes to prepare plus 1 hour refrigeration. Tart takes about 40 minutes to cook.

Variation
Substitute lobster for the whitefish for a special occasion or dinner party first course.

Freezing
Make the pastry in advance and wrap it very well. Label and freeze for up to 3 months. Defrost at room temperature before using. Also freeze uncooked in the flan dish.

MINESTRONE

Everyone's favorite Italian soup doesn't always
have to contain pasta. Our's substitutes potatoes
and is hearty enough to serve as a meal.

8oz dried white cannellini beans
2 tbsps olive oil
1 large ham bone, preferably prosciutto
1 onion, chopped
2 cloves garlic, crushed
4 sticks celery, sliced
2 carrots, diced
1 small head Savoy cabbage or 1lb fresh spinach, well washed
4oz green beans, cut into 1 inch lengths
8oz tomatoes, peeled, seeded and diced
1 dried red chili pepper
10 cups water (or half beef stock)
Salt and pepper
1 sprig fresh rosemary
1 bay leaf
3 potatoes, peeled and cut into small dice
3 zucchini, trimmed and cut into small dice
1 tbsp chopped fresh basil
1 tbsp chopped fresh parsley
Grated Parmesan cheese
Salt and pepper

1. Place the beans in a large bowl, cover with cold water and leave to soak overnight.

2. Heat the oil in a large stock pot and add ham bone, onion and garlic. Cook until onion has softened but not colored. Add the celery, carrots, cabbage and green beans. If using spinach, reserve until later.

3. Drain the beans and add them to the pot with the tomatoes and the chili pepper. Add the water and bring to the boil, skimming the surface as necessary. Add the rosemary and bay leaf and simmer, uncovered, until the beans are tender, about 1¼ hours.

4. Add the potatoes and cook for the further 20 minutes.

5. Add the zucchini and spinach and cook, skimming the surface, about 20 minutes longer. Remove the ham bone, rosemary and bay leaf and add basil and parsley. Serve with Parmesan cheese.

Step 1 Soak beans overnight in enough water to cover. They will swell in size.

Step 3 Using a metal spoon, skim any fat from the surface of the soup as it cooks.

Cook's Notes

 Time
Preparation takes about 20 minutes plus overnight soaking for the beans. Cooking takes about 2 hours.

 Watchpoint
The beans must be thoroughly cooked - it can be dangerous to eat them insufficiently cooked.

 Serving Ideas
If desired, cooked pasta may be substituted for the potatoes and added at the end of cooking time.

Variation
Other varieties of white beans may be used and canned beans may also be used. If using canned beans, add them with zucchini and spinach. Other vegetables such as broccoli, turnips, leeks or quartered Brussels sprouts, may be substituted.

SERVES 4-6

SPINACH GNOCCHI

Gnocchi are dumplings that are served like pasta. A dish of gnocchi can be served as a first course or as a light main course, sprinkled with cheese or accompanied by a sauce.

4oz chopped, frozen spinach
8oz ricotta cheese
3oz Parmesan cheese
Salt and pepper
Freshly grated nutmeg
1 egg, slightly beaten
3 tbsps butter

Step 3 Shape the gnocchi mixture with well-floured hands into ovals or balls.

Step 1 Press the spinach between two plates to remove excess moisture.

Step 5 Gnocchi will float to the surface of the water when cooked. Remove with a draining spoon.

1. Defrost the spinach and press it between two plates to extract all the moisture.

2. Mix the spinach with the ricotta cheese, half the Parmesan cheese, salt, pepper and nutmeg. Gradually add the egg, beating well until the mixture holds together when shaped.

3. With floured hands, form the mixture into oval shapes. Use about 1 tbsp mixture for each gnocchi.

4. Lower into simmering water, 3 or 4 at a time, and allow to

cook gently until the gnocchi float to the surface, about 1-2 minutes.

5. Remove with a draining spoon and place in a well buttered ovenproof dish.

6. When all the gnocchi are cooked, sprinkle on the remaining Parmesan cheese and dot with the remaining butter.

7. Reheat 10 minutes in a hot oven and brown under a pre-heated broiler before serving.

Cook's Notes

Time
Preparation takes about 15 minutes. cooking takes about 20 minutes.

Serving Ideas
Accompany with a tomato or cheese sauce for a light meal with a salad and hot bread.

Cook's Tip
Gnocchi are best served soon after they are cooked. If allowed to stand overnight they become very heavy.

SERVES 4

TOMATO SALAD RUSTICA

An informal salad with a country flavor, this is
perfect with barbecued meat, poultry or fish.

1lb tomatoes
1 onion
4-6 anchovies
Milk
2 tbsps capers
1 tsp chopped fresh oregano or basil
6 tbsps olive oil
1 tbsp lemon juice

Step 1 Remove the cores from the quartered tomatoes and slice again if large.

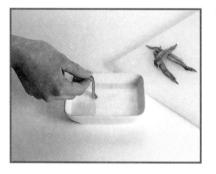

Step 1 Soak the anchovies in milk, rinse well and dry before using.

Step 2 Hold the onion with a fork to steady it while slicing into rings.

1. Soak the anchovies in a little milk before using, rinse, pat dry and chop. Cut the tomatoes into quarters and remove the cores. Slice each quarter in half again and place them in a serving bowl.

2. Slice the onion into rounds and then separate into rings. Scatter over the tomatoes. Cut the anchovies into small pieces and add to the tomatoes and onions along with the capers.

3. Mix the herbs, salt, pepper, oil and lemon juice together until well emulsified and pour over the salad. Mix all the ingredients gently and leave to stand for about 30 minutes before serving.

Cook's Notes

Cook's Tip
Soaking the anchovies in milk removes some of the strong taste and saltiness of the fish.

Time
Preparation takes about 20 minutes. Salad must stand for 30 minutes before serving.

Serving Ideas
Serve as a side dish with broiled meat, poultry or fish, or with a combination of other salads in an antipasti selection.

Variations
Use red onions or green onions for a change. Add sliced black olives if desired.

SERVES 4-6

PEPPER SALAD WITH CAPERS

Capers, the flower buds of a plant that flourishes in the warm
Italian climate, are a favorite ingredient in Italian cooking.

3 large peppers, red, green and yellow
6 tbsps olive oil
1 clove garlic, peeled and finely chopped
Basil leaves, roughly chopped
Fresh marjoram roughly chopped
2 tbsps capers
1 tbsp white wine vinegar

1. Cut the peppers in half and remove the core and seeds. Press with the palm of the hand or the back of a knife to flatten. Brush the skin side with oil and place the peppers under a preheated broiler.

2. Broil the peppers until the skins are well charred. Wrap in a towel and leave for 15 minutes. Unwrap and peel off the charred skin.

3. Cut the peppers into thick strips and arrange on a serving dish. Scatter over the chopped garlic, basil leaves, marjoram and capers.

4. Mix together the remaining olive oil with the vinegar and salt and pepper and pour over the salad. Refrigerate for 1 hour before serving.

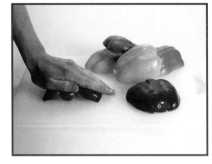

Step 1 Flatten the pepper halves with the palm of the hand or a large knife.

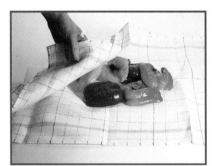

Step 2 Brush lightly with oil and broil until the skins are charred. Wrap in towels and leave for 15 minutes.

Cook's Notes

 Time
Preparation takes about 30 minutes plus 1 hour refrigeration.

 Preparation
The peppers may also be roasted in a hot oven for about 30 minutes. Alternatively, pierce whole peppers with a fork and hold them over a gas flame to char the skin.

 Watchpoint
The peppers must become very charred on the outside before the skin will peel well.

 Cook's Tip
Instead of chopping them, the basil leaves may be rolled up and cut into strips with kitchen scissors.

 Variation
The salad may be prepared with all red or all yellow peppers instead of the combination of the three colors. If using only red peppers, substitute red wine vinegar.

SERVES 6

SICILIAN CAPONATA

Vegetables, so important in Italian cuisine, are
often served separately. This combination makes an
excellent appetizer, vegetable course or accompaniment.

1 eggplant
Salt
½ cup olive oil
1 onion, sliced
2 sweet red peppers, cored, seeded and cut into
   1 inch pieces
2 sticks celery, sliced thickly
1lb canned plum tomatoes
2 tbsps red wine vinegar
1 tbsp sugar
1 clove garlic, crushed
12 black olives, pitted
1 tbsp capers
Salt and pepper

1. Cut the eggplant in half and score the cut surface.
Sprinkle with salt and leave to drain in a colander or on
paper towels for 30 minutes. Rinse, pat dry and cut into 1
inch cubes.

2. Heat the oil in a large sauté pan and add the onion,
peppers and celery. Lower the heat and cook for about 5
minutes, stirring occasionally. Add the eggplant and cook a
further 5 minutes.

3. Sieve the tomatoes to remove the seeds and add the
pulp and liquid to the vegetables in the sauté pan. Add the
remaining ingredients except the olives and capers and
cook for a further 2 minutes.

4. To remove the stones from the olives, roll them on a flat
surface to loosen the stones and then remove them with a
swivel vegetable peeler. Alternatively, use a cherry pitter.
Slice the olives in quarters and add to the vegetables with
the capers.

5. Simmer, uncovered, over moderate heat for 15 minutes
to evaporate most of the liquid. Adjust the seasoning and
serve hot or cold.

Step 1 Halve
eggplant and
score cut surface.
Sprinkle with salt
and leave to
drain.

Step 4 Roll black
olives on a flat
surface to loosen
stones.

Cook's Notes

Preparation
Scoring and salting the
eggplant helps remove any
bitter taste. Be sure to rinse all the salt
off before cooking.

Cook's Tip
When serving cold, caponata
may be prepared two days
in advance.

Serving Ideas
Caponata may be served as a
first course or in an antipasti
selection. Also serve as a side dish.

SERVES 6-8

FLAGEOLET, TUNA AND TOMATO SALAD

Tuna and tomatoes are two popular ingredients in Italian antipasto dishes.
Add beans, with their pale green color, for an attractive and easy first course or salad.

1lb canned flageolet beans (substitute white haricot
  beans or butter beans)
6oz canned tuna in oil
Juice of 1 lemon
Chopped fresh herbs (parsley, oregano, basil or
  marjoram)
8 tbsps olive oil
Salt and pepper
6-8 tomatoes, sliced

1. Drain the beans, rinse and leave in a colander to dry. Drain the tuna and flake it into a bowl.

2. Chop the herbs finely and mix with lemon juice, oil, salt and pepper. Add the beans to the tuna fish in the bowl and pour over the dressing, tossing carefully. Do not allow the tuna to break up too much.

3. Adjust the seasoning and pile the salad into a mound in a shallow serving dish. Cut the tomatoes into rounds about ¼ inch thick and place against the mound of salad. Serve immediately.

Step 2 Chop the herbs finely with a large knife using a mixture of different herbs, if desired.

Step 3 Mound the salad in the serving dish and place the tomatoes around it.

Cook's Notes

Time
Preparation takes about 15 minutes.

Serving Ideas
If desired, serve the salad on individual plates lined with radicchio or curly endive.

Variations
Add chopped green onions or red onions to the salad or add finely chopped garlic.

SERVES 4

SPIRALI WITH SPINACH AND BACON

Pasta doesn't have to have a sauce that cooks for hours.
This whole dish takes about 15 minutes. True Italian "fast food"!

12oz pasta spirals
8oz fresh spinach
3oz bacon
1 clove garlic, crushed
1 small red or green chili pepper
1 small red sweet pepper
1 small onion
3 tbsps olive oil
Salt and pepper

1. Cook the pasta in boiling salted water about 10-12 minutes or until just tender. Drain the pasta in a colander and rinse it under hot water. Keep the pasta in a bowl of water until ready to use.

2. Tear the stalks off the spinach and wash the leaves well, changing the water several times. Set aside to drain.

3. Remove the rind and bones from the bacon, if necessary, and dice the bacon finely. Cut the chili and the red pepper in half, remove the stems, core and seed, and slice finely. Slice the onion thinly.

4. Roll up several of the spinach leaves into a cigar shape and then shred them finely. Repeat until all the spinach is shredded.

5. Heat the oil in a sauté pan and add garlic, onion, peppers and bacon. Fry for 2 minutes, add the spinach and fry for a further 2 minutes, stirring continuously. Season with salt and pepper.

6. Drain the pasta spirals and toss them in a colander to remove excess water. Mix with the spinach sauce and serve immediately.

Step 2 Tear stalks off the spinach and wash the leaves well.

Step 3 Slice red pepper and chili pepper in half, remove seeds and core and shred finely with a large, sharp knife.

Step 4 Roll up the leaves in several layers to shred them faster.

Cook's Notes

 Time
Pasta takes about 10-12 minutes to cook. Sauce takes about 4 minutes to cook. Preparation takes about 20 minutes.

Preparation
Wash spinach leaves in cold water to keep them crisp, and change the water about three times to make sure all the grit is washed away.

 Watchpoint
Handle chilis with care and wash hands well after chopping chilis as the juice tends to stick to the skin.

SERVES 6

LASAGNE NAPOLETANA

This is lasagne as it is cooked and eaten in Naples.
With its layers of red, green and white it looks as delicious
as it tastes and is very easy to prepare and assemble.

9 sheets spinach lasagne pasta

Tomato Sauce

3 tbsps olive oil
2 cloves garlic, crushed
2lbs fresh tomatoes, peeled, or canned tomatoes,
    drained
2 tbsps chopped fresh basil, six whole leaves reserved
Salt and pepper
Pinch sugar

Cheese Filling

1lb ricotta cheese
4 tbsps unsalted butter
2 cups Mozzarella cheese, grated
Salt and pepper
Pinch nutmeg

1. Cook the pasta for 8 minutes in boiling salted water with 1 tbsp oil. Drain and rinse under hot water and place in a single layer on a damp cloth. Cover with another damp cloth and set aside.

2. To prepare the sauce, cook the garlic in remaining oil for about 1 minute in a large saucepan. When pale brown, add the tomatoes, basil, salt, pepper and sugar. If using fresh tomatoes, drop into boiling water for 6-8 seconds. Transfer to cold water and leave to cool completely. This will make the peels easier to remove.

3. Lower the heat under the saucepan and simmer the sauce for 35 minutes. Add more seasoning or sugar to taste.

4. Beat the ricotta cheese and butter together until creamy and stir into the remaining ingredients.

5. To assemble the lasagne, oil a rectangular baking dish and place 3 sheets of lasagne on the base. Cover with one third of the sauce and carefully spread on a layer of cheese. Place another 3 layers of pasta over the cheese and cover with another third of the sauce. Add the remaining cheese filling and cover with the remaining pasta. Spoon the remaining sauce on top.

6. Cover with foil and bake for 20 minutes at 375°F. Uncover and cook for 10 minutes longer. Garnish with the reserved leaves and leave to stand 10-15 minutes before serving.

Step 5 Place pasta on the base of an oiled baking dish. Spread tomato sauce over.

Step 5 Carefully spread the softened cheese mixture on top of the tomato sauce.

Cook's Notes

Cook's Tip
Lasagne can be assembled the day before and refrigerated. Allow 5-10 minutes more cooking time in the oven if not at room temperature.

Time
Preparation takes about 25 minutes, cooking takes about 1-1¼ hours.

Variations
Use plain pasta instead, if desired. If using pre-cooked lasagne pasta, follow the baking times in the package directions.

SERVES 4

PENNE WITH HAM AND ASPARAGUS

The Italian word penne means quills,
due to the diagonal cut on both ends.

8oz penne
12oz fresh asparagus
4oz cooked ham
2 tbsps butter or margarine
1 cup heavy cream

Step 1 Peel the asparagus stalks with a swivel vegetable peeler.

1. Using a swivel vegetable peeler, scrape the sides of the asparagus spears starting about 2 inches from the top. Cut off the ends of the spears about 1 inch from the bottom.

2. Cut the ham into strips about ½ inch thick.

3. Bring a sauté pan of water to the boil, adding a pinch of salt. Move the pan so it is half on and half off direct heat. Place in the asparagus spears so that the tips are off the heat. Cover the pan and bring back to the boil. Cook the asparagus spears for about 2 minutes. Drain and allow to cool.

4. Cut the asparagus into 1 inch lengths, leaving the tips whole.

5. Melt the butter in the sauté pan and add the asparagus and ham. Cook briefly to evaporate the liquid, and add the cream. Bring to the boil and cook for about 5 minutes to thicken the cream.

6. Meanwhile, cook the pasta in boiling salted water with 1 tbsp oil for about 10-12 minutes.

7. Drain the pasta and rinse under hot water. Toss in a colander to drain and mix with the sauce. Serve with grated Parmesan cheese, if desired.

Step 4 Cut ham and cooked asparagus into 1 inch lengths. Leave the asparagus tips whole.

Step 5 Boil the cream with the asparagus and ham for about 5 minutes to thicken.

Cook's Notes

Time
Pasta takes 10-12 minutes to cook. Sauce takes about 8 minutes to cook. Preparation takes about 20 minutes.

Variations
If using frozen instead of fresh asparagus, do not peel or pre-cook. Substitute broccoli spears for the asparagus and prepare in the same way. If using peas instead of asparagus, cook them in the butter with the ham, add the cream and cook 5 minutes.

Serving Ideas
May be served as a first course in smaller amounts.

SERVES 4

SPAGHETTI AMATRICIANA

This is another quickly cooked sauce with a rich, spicy taste.
Use less of the chili pepper for a less fiery flavor.

1 onion
6 strips Canadian bacon
1lb ripe tomatoes
1 red chili pepper
1½ tbsps oil
12oz spaghetti

1. Slice the onion thinly. Remove rind from the bacon and cut into thin strips.

2. Drop the tomatoes into boiling water for 6-8 seconds. Remove with a draining spoon and place in cold water, and leave to cool completely. This will make the peels easier to remove.

3. When the tomatoes are peeled, cut them in half and remove the seeds and pulp with a teaspoon. Rub the seeds and pulp through a strainer and retain juice to use in the sauce if desired. Chop the tomato flesh roughly and set it aside.

4. Cut the stem off the chili pepper and cut the pepper in half lengthwise. Remove the seeds and core and cut the pepper into thin strips. Cut the strips into small dice.

5. Heat the oil in a sauté pan and add the onion and bacon. Stir over medium heat for about 5 minutes, until the onion is transparent. Drain off excess fat and add the tomatoes and chili and mix well. Simmer the sauce gently, uncovered, for about 5 minutes, stirring occasionally.

6. Meanwhile, cook the spaghetti in boiling salted water with 1 tbsp oil for about 10-12 minutes. Drain and rinse in hot water and toss in a colander to dry. To serve, spoon the sauce on top of the spaghetti and sprinkle with freshly grated Parmesan cheese, if desired.

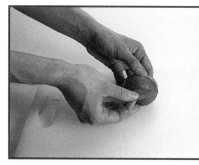

Step 2 Placing tomatoes in boiling water and then in cold water makes the skins easier to remove.

Step 3 Cut the peeled tomatoes in half and remove the seeds and pulp with a teaspoon. Cut the flesh roughly.

Step 4 Remove the stems, seeds and cores from the chili pepper, cut into thin strips and then chop into fine dice.

Cook's Notes

Time
Spaghetti takes about 10-12 minutes to cook, sauce takes about 8 minutes to cook, preparation takes about 20-25 minutes.

Cook's Tip
It is not necessary to use the whole chili pepper; use as much as desired.

Watchpoint
Wash hands very well after handling chili peppers or use rubber gloves while chopping them.

SERVES 4

HOME~MADE TAGLIATELLE WITH SUMMER SAUCE

Pasta making is not as difficult as you might think.
It is well worth it, too, because home-made pasta is in a class by itself.

Pasta Dough

1 cup all-purpose flour
1 cup bread flour
2 large eggs
2 tsps olive oil
Pinch salt

Sauce

1lb unpeeled tomatoes, seeded and cut into small dice
1 large green pepper, cored, seeded and cut in small dice
1 onion, cut in small dice
1 tbsps chopped fresh basil
1 tbsp chopped fresh parsley
2 cloves garlic, crushed
½ cup olive oil and vegetable oil mixed

1. Place the flours in a mound on a work surface and make a well in the center. Place the eggs, oil and salt in the center of the well.

2. Using a fork, beat the ingredients in the center to blend them and gradually incorporate the flour from the outside edge. The dough may also be mixed in a food processor.

3. When half the flour is incorporated, start kneading using the palms of the hands and not the fingers.. This may also be done in a food processor. Cover the dough and leave it to rest for 15 minutes.

4. Divide the dough in quarters and roll out thinly with a rolling pin on a floured surface or use a pasta machine, dusting dough lightly with flour before rolling. If using a machine, follow the manufacturer's directions. Allow the sheets of pasta to dry for about 10 minutes on a floured

surface or on tea towels. Cut the sheets into strips about ¼ inch wide by hand or machine, dusting lightly with flour while cutting. Leave the cut pasta to dry while preparing the sauce.

5. Combine all the sauce ingredients, mixing well. Cover and refrigerate overnight.

6. Cook the pasta for 5-6 minutes in boiling salted water with a spoonful of oil. Drain the pasta and rinse under very hot water. Toss in a colander to drain excess water. Place the hot pasta in serving dish. Pour the cold sauce over and toss.

Step 3 Knead with palms of hands to bring dough together until smooth.

Step 4 Roll the dough out thinly and cut into thin strips.

Cook's Notes

 Time
Preparation takes about 30 minutes, cooking takes about 5-6 minutes.

 Watchpoint
Pasta must remain very hot to balance the cold sauce.

 **Serving Ideas**
This basic pasta recipe can be used with other shapes of pasta such as lasagne, cannelloni, ravioli, farfalle (butterflies or bows), or cut into very fine noodles.

SERVES 4

PIZZA WITH PEPPERS, OLIVES & ANCHOVIES

Pizza really needs no introduction. It originated in Naples
and has been adopted everywhere. Change the toppings to suit your taste.

Pizza Dough

½oz fresh yeast
½ tsp sugar
¾ cup lukewarm water
2 cups all-purpose flour
Pinch salt
2 tbsps oil

Topping

2 tsps olive oil
1 onion, finely chopped
1 clove garlic, crushed
1lb canned tomatoes
1 tbsp tomato paste
½ tsp each oregano and basil
1 tsp sugar
Salt and pepper
½ red pepper
½ green pepper
½ cup black olives, pitted
2oz canned anchovies, drained
1 cup Mozzarella cheese, grated
2 tbsp grated Parmesan cheese

1. Cream the yeast with the sugar in a small bowl, add the lukewarm water and leave to stand for 10 minutes to prove. Bubbles will appear on the surface when ready.

2. Sift flour and salt into a bowl, make a well in the center and add the oil and the yeast mixture. Using a wooden spoon, beat the liquid in the center of the well, gradually incorporating the flour from the outside until it forms a firm dough.

3. Turn the dough out onto a floured surface and knead for 10 minutes, or until the dough is smooth and elastic. Place in a lightly oiled bowl or in a large plastic bag, cover or tie the bag and leave to stand in a warm place for 30 minutes, or until the dough has doubled in bulk.

4. Knock the dough back and knead it into a smooth ball. Flatten the dough and roll out into a circle on a floured surface. The circle should be about 10 inches in diameter.

5. To prepare the topping, heat the oil in a heavy-based saucepan and add the onion and the garlic. Cook until the onion and garlic have softened but not colored. Add the tomatoes and their juice, tomato paste, herbs, sugar, salt and pepper. Bring the sauce to the boil and then allow to simmer, uncovered, to reduce. Stir the sauce occasionally to prevent sticking. When the sauce is thick and smooth, leave it to cool. Spread the cooled sauce over the pizza dough. Sprinkle half the cheese on top of the tomato sauce and then arrange the topping ingredients. Sprinkle with remaining cheese and bake in a 400°F oven for 15-20 minutes or until the cheese is melted and bubbling and the crust is brown.

Step 4 When the dough has doubled in bulk, knock back before kneading again lightly.

Cook's Notes

Time
Dough takes about 40 minutes to make, including the rising. The tomato sauce needs to cook for 10-15 minutes. Pizza takes 15-20 minutes to bake.

Variations
Other ingredients, such as Italian hams and sausages, fish and shellfish, capers, green olives, or zucchini, may be used as toppings.

SERVES 4-6

PIZZA RUSTICA

This farmhouse pie is really a cross between quiche
and pizza. Whichever you think it resembles most,
there is no question that it is delicious.

Pizza Dough

(see recipe for Pizza with Peppers, Olives and Anchovies)

Filling

Grated Parmesan cheese
4oz prosciutto or Parma ham, sliced
2 tomatoes, peeled, seeded and roughly chopped
2oz Mozzarella cheese, diced
1 tbsp chopped fresh parsley
1 tbsp chopped fresh basil
2 eggs, lightly beaten
5 tbsps heavy cream
2oz Fontina cheese, finely grated
Pinch nutmeg
Salt and pepper

Step 2 Roll out the dough, place in a dish and press up the sides to form an edge.

1. Prepare the dough as for the Pizza with Peppers, Olives and Anchovies. When the dough has doubled in bulk, knock it back and knead lightly. Flatten the dough into a circle or rectangle and roll out. Roll to a circle about 10 inches in diameter or a rectangle about 11x7 inches.

2. Lightly oil the baking dish, place in the dough and press out with floured fingertips to form a raised edge on the sides of the dish.

3. Sprinkle the base of the dough with some of the Parmesan cheese and place on a layer of ham. Cover the ham with the chopped tomato. Mix the remaining ingredients together and pour over the tomato and ham.

4. Bake on the lowest shelf of the oven for about 35 minutes at 375°F. The top of the pizza should be nicely browned and the edge of the dough should be golden when the pizza is ready. Serve hot.

Step 3 Fill with Parmesan, ham and tomatoes.

Step 3 Mix cream, cheese and eggs together and pour onto the pizza.

Cook's Notes

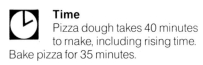

Time
Pizza dough takes 40 minutes to make, including rising time. Bake pizza for 35 minutes.

Freezing
Pizzas can be prepared and frozen in their unbaked form. When cooking from frozen, allow an extra 10 minutes. Pizza dough bases may also be frozen unfilled. Allow to defrost before topping.

Variations
If Fontina cheese is not available, substitute Gruyère or Emmental. Vary the filling ingredients using different vegetables and meats as desired.

SERVES 4-6

LIVER VENEZIANA

As the name indicates, this recipe originated
in Venice. The lemon juice offsets the rich
taste of liver in this very famous Italian dish.

Risotto

9oz Italian rice
3 tbsps butter or margarine
1 large onion, chopped
4 tbsps dry white wine
2 cups chicken stock
¼ tsp saffron
2 tbsps grated fresh Parmesan cheese
Salt and pepper

Liver

1lb calves' or lambs' liver
Flour for dredging
3 onions, thinly sliced
2 tbsps butter or margarine
3 tbsps oil
Salt and pepper
Juice of ½ a lemon
1 tbsp chopped parsley

1. Melt the butter for the risotto in a large sauté pan, add the onion and cook until soft but not colored, over gentle heat.

2. Add the rice and cook for about a minute until the rice looks clear.

3. Add the wine, stock, saffron and seasoning. Stir well and bring to the boil. Lower the heat and cook gently, stirring frequently until the liquid has evaporated. This will take about 20 minutes.

4. Meanwhile, skin the liver and cut out any large tubes.

5. Cut the liver into strips and toss in a sieve with the flour to coat.

6. Heat the butter or margarine and 1 tbsp oil in a large sauté or frying pan. Cook the onions until golden. Remove the onions from the pan to a plate. Add more oil if necessary, raise the heat under the pan and add the liver. Cook, stirring constantly, for about 2 minutes. Return the onions and add the lemon juice and parsley. Cook a further 2 minutes or until the liver is done. Season with salt and pepper and serve with the risotto.

7. To finish the risotto, add the cheese and salt and pepper to taste when the liquid has evaporated, and toss to melt the cheese.

Step 3 Lower the heat and cook gently, stirring frequently until the liquid has evaporated.

Step 5 Cut the liver into strips and toss with flour in a sieve to coat each piece evenly.

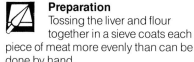

Cook's Notes

Time
Risotto takes about 30 minutes to prepare and cook. Liver takes about 4 minutes to cook.

Watchpoint
Liver and all organ meats need quick cooking or they will toughen.

Preparation
Tossing the liver and flour together in a sieve coats each piece of meat more evenly than can be done by hand.

Cook's Tip
If desired, add 4 tbsps stock to the recipe for a little more sauce.

SERVES 4

VEAL SCALOPPINE WITH PROSCIUTTO AND CHEESE

Veal is the meat used most often in Italian cooking. Good veal is tender and quick cooking, but expensive. Save this recipe for your next dinner party!

8 veal escalopes
2 tbsps butter or margarine
1 clove garlic, crushed
1 sprig rosemary
8 slices prosciutto ham
8 slices Mozzarella cheese
3 tbsps sherry
½ cup beef stock
Salt and pepper

Step 3 Place a slice of ham on top of each slice of veal and pour over the sherry and stock and add the rosemary.

Step 2 Cook the veal on both sides until lightly browned.

Step 6 Place the meat under a preheated broiler and cook to melt the cheese and lightly brown the top.

1. Pound the veal escalopes out thinly between two pieces of wax paper with a meat mallet or a rolling pin.

2. Melt the butter or margarine in a sauté pan and add the veal and garlic. Cook until the veal is lightly browned on both sides.

3. Place a piece of prosciutto on top of each piece of veal and add the sherry, stock and sprig of rosemary to the pan. Cover the pan and cook the veal for about 10 minutes over

gentle heat, or until done.

4. Remove the meat to a heatproof serving dish and top each piece of veal with a slice of cheese.

5. Bring the cooking liquid from the veal to the boil and allow to boil rapidly to reduce slightly.

6. Meanwhile, broil the veal to melt and brown the cheese. Remove the sprig of rosemary from the sauce and pour the sauce around the meat to serve.

Cook's Notes

Time
Preparation takes about 15 minutes, cooking takes 15-20 minutes.

Variations
White wine may be substituted for the sherry, if desired. 1 tsp of tomato paste may be added to the sauce. Use chicken, turkey or pork instead of the veal.

SERVES 4-8

PORK ROULADES WITH POLENTA

Polenta, either boiled or fried, is a staple dish in
Italy as potatoes are elsewhere in the world.

8oz coarse yellow cornmeal
6 cups chicken stock
Salt and white pepper

Roulades

8 pork escalopes or steaks
8 slices Parma ham
4 large cup mushrooms
4 tbsps grated Parmesan cheese
1 tbsp chopped fresh sage
Seasoned flour for dredging
4 tbsps olive oil
1 small onion, finely chopped
2 sticks celery, finely chopped
1 clove garlic, crushed
6 tbsps brown stock
½ cup dry white wine
4oz canned plum tomatoes, drained and juice reserved
1 tsp tomato paste
Salt and pepper
6 tbsps dry Marsala
Fresh sage leaves for garnish

1. Bring the chicken stock for the polenta to the boil in a
large stock pot and start adding the cornmeal in a very slow,
steady stream, stirring continuously. Add salt and pepper
and continue cooking over very low heat, stirring
frequently, for about 55 minutes.

2. Flatten the pork escalopes or steaks and place a slice of
Parma ham on top of each. Chop the mushrooms and
divide among the pork escalopes, spooning on top of the
ham slices. Sprinkle over the Parmesan cheese and the
fresh sage.

3. Fold the sides of the pork escalopes into the center to
seal them, and roll up the pork jelly roll fashion. Secure each
roll with a wooden pick stick. Dredge each roulade in flour,
shaking off the excess.

4. Heat the olive oil in a large sauté pan or frying pan and
add the pork roulades, seam side down first. Cook on all
sides until nicely browned. Remove the roulades and keep
them warm.

5. Add the onion and celery to the oil in the pan and cook
until lightly browned. Add the garlic and all the remaining
ingredients except the Marsala. Reserve the juice from the
tomatoes for later use if necessary. Bring the sauce to the
boil, breaking up the tomatoes. Return the roulades to the
pan, cover and cook over moderate heat for about 15-20
minutes or until the pork is completely cooked. Add
reserved tomato juice, as necessary, if liquid is drying out.

6. When the pork is cooked, remove to a dish and keep it
warm. Add the Marsala to the sauce and bring to the boil.
Allow to boil 5-10 minutes. The sauce may be puréed in a
food processor and also sieved if desired.

7. To assemble the dish, spoon the polenta on a serving
plate. Remove the wooden picks from the roulades and
place on top of the polenta. Spoon the sauce over the meat
and garnish the dish with fresh sage leaves.

Step 2 Place all
the filling
ingredients on top
of the pork
scallops, fold in
the sides and roll
up. Secure with
wooden picks.

Cook's Notes

Time
Polenta takes almost 1 hour to
cook. Roulades will take about
20 minutes to prepare and 20 minutes
to cook.

Watchpoint
Be sure to stir the polenta
often and add more liquid if it
begins to dry out as it can easily stick to
the pan.

Variations
Double the quantity of
cornmeal and cut the cooking
time down to 30-35 minutes. Spoon
into a lightly oiled pan and allow to
cool. This version of polenta can be cut
into squares and fried in hot oil. Serve
as an accompaniment to any meat.

SERVES 6-8

CRESPELLE ALLA BOLOGNESE

Almost all countries in the world have a kind of
pancake, and crespelle are the Italian version. Use
other fillings and sauces for lots of variety.

Bolognese Filling

2 tbsps butter or margarine
1 tbsp olive oil
2 onions, finely chopped
8oz ground beef
1 small green pepper, seeded, cored and finely chopped
4oz canned plum tomatoes
1 tbsp tomato paste
½ cup beef stock
1 bay leaf
2 tsps chopped basil
1 tsp chopped oregano
2 tbsps sherry
Salt and pepper

Crespelle Batter

3 eggs
1 cup all-purpose flour
Pinch salt
1 cup water
2 tsps olive oil
Melted butter

Tomato sauce

1 tbsp butter or margarine
1 clove garlic, crushed
1 onion, finely chopped
1lb canned plum tomatoes
Salt, pepper and a pinch of sugar
Fresh basil leaves

1. Heat the butter and oil in a deep saucepan for the
Bolognese filling. Put in the onion and cook slowly until soft
but not colored. Increase the heat and add the beef. Stir
the beef while cooking, until all the meat is brown. Add
chopped pepper, tomatoes and their juice, tomato paste,
stock, herbs, salt and pepper to taste and simmer gently for
about 45 minutes or until the mixture thickens, stirring
occasionally. Add the sherry and cook for a further 5
minutes and set aside.

2. Sift the flour for the crespelle with a pinch of salt. Break
the eggs into a bowl and beat to mix thoroughly. Mix the
flour into the eggs gradually, beating all the time until the
mixture is smooth. Add water and the oil and stir in well.
Cover the bowl with a damp cloth and leave in a cool place
for 30 minutes.

3. Heat the crêpe pan or a 7 inch frying pan. Lightly
grease with the melted butter and pour a large spoonful of
the batter into the center of the pan. Swirl the pan to coat the
base evenly. Fry until the crespelle is brown on the
underside, loosen the edge with a pallete knife, and turn
over and brown the other side. Stack and wrap in a clean
towel until needed.

4. To make the tomato sauce, melt the butter in a small
saucepan and cook garlic and onion slowly for about 5
minutes, or until softened but not colored. Reserve whole
basil leaves for garnish and chop 2 tsps. Add the tomatoes
to the onions and garlic along with the basil, salt, pepper
and a pinch of sugar. Cook for about 10-15 minutes or until
the onions are completely soft. Drain to remove the seeds,
pressing the pulp against the strainer to extract as much
liquid as possible.

5. To assemble, lay the crespelle out on a large, clean work
surface and put 2 heaped spoonfuls of Bolognese filling
into each. Roll up and place in an ovenproof dish. Repeat
until all the crespelle have been filled.

6. Put into a 400°F oven and heat for about 8 minutes.
Heat the tomato sauce and spoon over the crespelle before
serving. Garnish with basil leaves and serve immediately.

Time
Preparation takes about 45
minutes, cooking takes about
1 hour 15 minutes.

Preparation
The crespelle batter must
stand for 30 minutes to allow
the starch to swell for the batter to
thicken properly.

Variations
Crespelle can be used with a
variety of fillings and toppings,
both sweet and savory.

SERVES 4-6

CHICKEN CACCIATORE

The name means Chicken the Hunter's Way, and that means the addition of mushrooms. Though not traditional, pasta is a good accompaniment.

3 tbsps oil
4oz mushrooms, quartered, if large
3lb chicken, skinned if desired and cut into pieces
1 onion
2 cloves garlic
½ cup vermouth
1 tbsp white wine vinegar
½ cup chicken stock
1 tsp oregano
1 sprig fresh rosemary
1lb canned tomatoes
2oz black olives, pitted
2 tbsps chopped parsley
Salt and pepper

1. Heat the oil in a heavy-based frying pan and cook the mushrooms for about 1-2 minutes. Remove them and set aside. Brown the chicken in the oil and transfer the browned pieces to an ovenproof casserole.

2. Chop the onion and garlic finely. Pour off all but 1 tbsp of the oil in the frying pan and reheat the pan. Cook the onion and garlic until softened but not colored. Add the vermouth and vinegar, and boil to reduce by half. Add the chicken stock, tomatoes, oregano, rosemary, salt and pepper. Break up the tomatoes and bring the sauce to the boil. Allow to cook for 2 minutes.

3. Pour the sauce over the chicken in the casserole, cover and cook at 350°F for about 1 hour.

4. To remove the stones from the olives, roll them on a flat surface to loosen the stones and then use a swivel vegetable peeler to extract them. Alternatively, use a cherry pitter.

5. Add mushrooms and olives during the last 5 minutes of cooking.

Step 2 Cut onion in half lengthwise leaving the root end intact. Holding the knife parallel to the chopping board, cut the onion in thin horizontal slices, but not through to the root end.

Step 2 Cut the onion lengthwise in thin strips, leaving the onion attached at the root end.

Step 2 Cut cross-wise through the onion; the onion will fall apart into small dice.

6. Remove the rosemary before serving, and sprinkle with chopped parsley.

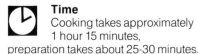
Cook's Notes

 Time
Cooking takes approximately 1 hour 15 minutes, preparation takes about 25-30 minutes.

Cook's Tip
Pitted black olives are available in some delicatessens.

Serving Idea
Serve with spaghetti or pasta shapes and sprinkle with grated Parmesan cheese.

SERVES 4

TURKEY MARSALA

Marsala is a dessert wine from Sicily which complements chicken, veal or turkey surprisingly well. It is traditional, but sherry will serve as a substitute if Marsala is unavailable.

4 turkey breast fillets or escalopes
4 tbsps butter or margarine
1 clove garlic
4 anchovy fillets, soaked in milk
Capers
4 slices Mozzarella cheese
2 tsps chopped marjoram
1 tbsp chopped parsley
3 tbsps Marsala
½ cup heavy cream
Salt and pepper

1. Flatten the turkey breasts between two sheets of wax paper with a meat mallet or rolling pin if necessary.

2. Melt butter in a sauté pan and, when foaming, add the garlic and the turkey. Cook for a few minutes on each side until lightly browned. Remove them from the pan.

3. Drain the anchovy fillets and rinse them well. Dry on paper towels. Put a slice of cheese on top of each turkey fillet and arrange the anchovies and capers on top of each. Sprinkle with the chopped herbs and return the turkey to the pan.

4. Cook the turkey a further 5 minutes over moderate heat, until the turkey is done and the cheese has melted. Remove to a serving dish and keep warm. Return the pan to the heat and add the Marsala. Scrape the browned pan juices off the bottom and reduce the heat. Add the cream and whisk in well. Lower the heat and simmer gently, uncovered, for a few minutes to thicken the sauce. Season the sauce with salt and pepper and spoon over the turkey fillets to serve.

Step 1 Flatten the turkey breasts between two sheets of wax paper with a rolling pin or meat mallet.

Step 3 Place a slice of cheese on top of each turkey breast and top with anchovies, capers and herbs.

Step 4 Cook until turkey is done and the cheese has melted.

Cook's Notes

Time
Preparation takes about 25 minutes and cooking about 15 minutes.

Watchpoint
Turkey breast fillets are very lean so can dry out easily if over-cooked.

Serving Suggestions
Accompany the Turkey Marsala with new potatoes and lightly cooked zucchini.

SERVES 6

TURKEY KEBABS

You don't have to buy a whole turkey for these! Small portions are now readily available at supermarkets and butchers.

3lbs turkey meat
2 tsps chopped sage
1 sprig rosemary
Juice of 1 lemon
2 tbsps olive oil
Salt and pepper
4oz bacon, rinds and bones removed
Whole sage leaves

Step 2 Stretch the bacon by scraping it with the blunt side of a knife.

Step 1 Remove the turkey bones and cut the meat into small, even-sized pieces.

Step 3 Cut the bacon into halves and wrap around a piece of turkey. Thread the ingredients onto skewers.

1. Remove any bones from the turkey and cut the meat into even-sized pieces. Combine the chopped sage, rosemary, lemon juice, oil, salt and pepper in a large bowl and add the turkey meat. Stir once or twice to coat evenly, cover and leave in the refrigerator overnight.

2. Cut the bacon in half and wrap around some of the pieces of turkey. Leave other pieces of turkey unwrapped.

3. Thread the bacon, wrapped turkey, plain turkey and whole sage leaves onto skewers, alternating the ingredients.

4. Cook in a preheated 400°F oven for about 40 minutes. Alternatively, cook for 30 minutes and place the kebabs under a preheated broiler for 10 minutes to crisp the bacon. Baste frequently with the marinade while cooking. Pour any remaining marinade and pan juices over the kebabs to serve.

Cook's Notes

Time
Kebabs take about 20 minutes to assemble and need to marinate overnight. Cooking takes about 40 minutes.

Serving Ideas
Serve with a green salad, fried polenta or risotto.

Variation
Use chicken, if desired.

SERVES 4-6

SWORDFISH KEBABS

Swordfish is one of the most commonly caught fish
in Southern Italy and Sicily. It won't fall apart
during cooking – a bonus when making kebabs.

2¼lbs swordfish steaks
6 tbsps olive oil
1 tsp chopped oregano
1 tsp chopped marjoram
Juice and rind of ½ a lemon
4 tomatoes, cut in thick slices
2 lemons, cut in thin slices
Salt and freshly ground pepper
Lemon slices and Italian parsley for garnish

1. Cut the swordfish steaks into 2 inch pieces.

2. Mix the olive oil, herbs, lemon juice and rind together and set it aside. Thread the swordfish, tomato slices and lemon slices on skewers, alternating the ingredients. Brush the skewers with the oil and lemon juice mixture and cook under a preheated broiler for about 10 minutes, basting frequently with the lemon and oil. Serve garnished with lemons and parsley.

Step 1 Cut the swordfish steaks into even-sized pieces.

Step 2 Thread the ingredients onto the skewers, alternating the colors.

Cook's Notes

Time
Preparation takes about 15 minutes, cooking takes about 10 minutes.

Variations
Fresh tuna may be used instead of swordfish. Use cherry tomatoes instead of sliced tomatoes, if available.

Serving Ideas
Accompany the kebabs with risotto and a green salad.

SERVES 4

RED MULLET WITH HERB & MUSHROOM SAUCE

This is a Mediterranean fish with a slight taste of prawns.
It is often cooked with the liver left in − a delicacy.

1lb small mushrooms, left whole
1 clove garlic, finely chopped
3 tbsps olive oil
Juice of 1 lemon
1 tbsp finely chopped parsley
2 tsps finely chopped basil
1 tsp finely chopped marjoram or sage
4 tbsps dry white wine mixed with ½ tsp cornstarch
Few drops anchovy paste
4 red mullet, each weighing about 8oz
2 tsps white breadcrumbs
2 tsps freshly grated Parmesan cheese

1. Combine the mushrooms, garlic and olive oil in a small frying pan. Cook over moderate heat for about 1 minute, until the garlic and mushrooms are slightly softened. Add all the herbs, lemon juice and white wine and cornstarch mixture. Bring to the boil and cook until thickened. Add anchovy paste to taste. Set aside while preparing the fish.

2. To clean the fish, cut along the stomach from the gills to the vent, the small hole near the tail. Clean out the cavity of the fish, leaving the liver, if desired.

3. To remove the gills, lift the flap and snip them out with a sharp pair of scissors. Rinse the fish well and pat dry.

4. Place the fish head to tail in a shallow ovenproof dish that can be used for serving. The fish should fit snugly into the dish.

5. Pour the prepared sauce over the fish and sprinkle with the breadcrumbs and Parmesan cheese.

6. Cover the dish loosely with foil and cook in the preheated oven at 375°F, for about 20 minutes. Uncover for the last 5 minutes, if desired, and raise the oven temperature slightly. This will lightly brown the fish.

Step 3 Lift the flap over the gills and use kitchen scissors to snip the gills away.

Step 4 Place the fish head to tail in a shallow baking dish just large enough to accommodate them.

Cook's Notes

 Time
Preparation takes about 30 minutes, cooking takes about 5 minutes for the sauce and 20 minutes for the fish.

Preparation
If the fish need to be scaled, use the blunt edge of a knife and scrape from the tail to the head. Rinse well and remove any loose scales. The fishmonger will gut the fish, scale them and remove the gills if desired.

 Variations
Use other fish such as bream or sardines.

SERVES 4

FISH MILANESE

These fish, cooked in the style of
Milan, have a crispy crumb coating
and the fresh tang of lemon juice.

8 sole or plaice fillets
2 tbsps dry vermouth
1 bay leaf
6 tbsps olive oil
Salt and pepper
Seasoned flour for dredging
2 eggs, lightly beaten
Dry breadcrumbs
Oil for shallow frying
6 tbsps butter
1 clove garlic, crushed
2 tsps chopped parsley
2 tbsps capers
1 tsp chopped fresh oregano
Juice of 1 lemon
Salt and pepper
Lemon wedges and parsley to garnish

1. Skin the fillets with a sharp filleting knife. Remove any small bones and place the fillets in a large, shallow dish. Combine the vermouth, oil and bay leaf in a small saucepan and heat gently. Allow to cool completely and pour over the fish. Leave the fish to marinate for about 1 hour, turning them occasionally.

2. Remove the fish from the marinade and dredge lightly with the seasoned flour.

3. Dip the fillets into the beaten eggs to coat, or use a pastry brush to brush the eggs onto the fillets. Dip the egg-coated fillet into the breadcrumbs, pressing the crumbs on firmly.

4. Heat the oil in a large frying pan. Add the fillets and cook slowly on both sides until golden brown. Cook for about 3 minutes on each side, remove and drain on paper towels.

5. Pour the oil out of the frying pan and wipe it clean. Add the butter and the garlic and cook until both turn a light brown. Add the herbs, capers and lemon juice and pour immediately over the fish. Garnish with lemon wedges and sprigs of parsley.

Step 1 Hold each fillet firmly by the tail end and work a sharp filleting knife down the length of the fillet, holding the knife at a slight angle. Keep the blade as close as possible to the fish.

Step 3 Dip or brush the fillets with the beaten egg and press on the breadcrumb coating firmly.

Cook's Notes

 Time
Preparation takes 1 hour for the fish to marinate, cooking takes about 6 minutes. It may be necessary to cook the fish in several batches, depending upon the size of the frying pan.

 Cook's Tip
If necessary, keep the fish fillets warm by placing on a wire cooling rack covered with paper towels and place in a warm oven, leaving the door slightly ajar. Sprinkling the fish fillets lightly with salt as they drain on paper towels helps remove some of the oil.

 Variations
Other whitefish fillets may be prepared in the same way. Choose fillets that are of even size so that they cook in the same length of time. Chopped onion may be substituted for the garlic, if desired.

SERVES 4

CARAMEL ORANGES

This is one of the classic Italian sweets.
Vary the darkness of the caramel to suit
your taste, but watch it carefully!

4 large oranges
1¼ cups sugar
1½ cups water
¼ cup extra water
2 tbsps brandy or orange liqueur

1. Use a swivel vegetable peeler to peel thin strips from two of the oranges. Take off any white pith and cut the strips into very thin julienne strips with a sharp knife.

2. Place the julienne strips in a small saucepan, cover with water and bring to the boil.

3. Peel all the oranges with a serrated-edged knife. Cut the ends off first and then take the peel and pith off in very thin strips using a sawing motion. Cut the oranges horizontally into slices about ¼ inch thick. Drain the orange peel strips and leave to dry. Combine sugar and water in a heavy-based pan. Reserve ¼ cup water for later use. Place the mixture over medium heat until the sugar has dissolved. Add the drained orange peel strips to the pan.

4. Boil the syrup gently, uncovered, for about 10 minutes or until the orange strips are glazed. Remove the strips from the pan and place on a lightly oiled plate.

5. Return the pan to high heat and allow the syrup to boil, uncovered, until it turns a pale golden brown. Remove from the heat immediately and quickly add the extra water. Return to gentle heat and cook for a few minutes to dissolve hardened sugar. Remove the pan from the heat and allow to cool completely. Stir in the brandy.

6. Arrange the orange slices in a serving dish and pour over the cooled syrup. Pile the glazed orange strips on top and refrigerate for several hours, or overnight, before serving.

Step 1 Peel the oranges into thin strips with a vegetable peeler. Remove any white pith and cut into thin julienne strips.

Step 3 Use a serrated knife to take off orange peel in thin strips.

Step 5 Cook the sugar and water to a pale golden brown syrup.

Cook's Notes

Time
Preparation takes about 25 minutes, cooking takes about 10 minutes to parboil the orange strips and about 10-15 minutes to caramelize the syrup.

Watchpoint
Keep a close eye on the syrup as it is caramelizing. It can burn very quickly.

Cook's Tip
All the white pith must be removed from the oranges and the orange strips or the whole dish will taste bitter.

SERVES 4-8

CHESTNUT & ALMOND STUFFED PEACHES

A favorite sweet in Milan during the peach season.

4 large freestone peaches
1 cup dry white wine
2 tbsps brandy

Filling

2oz semi-sweet chocolate
2¾oz chestnut spread
1 egg yolk
1 tbsp ground almonds
1 tbsp peach liqueur or brandy
½ cup heavy cream
4 amaretti or ratafia biscuits

Step 4 Fold whipped cream into the chocolate-chestnut mixture along with the almonds.

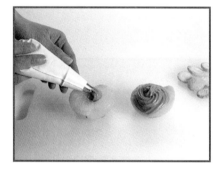

Step 6 Pipe the filling into the hollow in each peach half.

Step 1 Remove the peach stones using a small knife or swivel vegetable peeler.

1. Wash the peaches, peel them and cut them in half. Carefully remove the stones and place the peaches in a large bowl with the wine, brandy and enough water to cover them completely. Marinate for 1 hour.

2. Cut the chocolate into small pieces and melt in the top of a double boiler. Stir in the chestnut spread. Remove the chocolate from the heat and leave to cool for about 2 minutes, stirring frequently.

3. Beat in the egg yolk until well incorporated. Add the

peach liqueur or brandy and stir well. Allow to cool.

4. Whip the cream and fold into the chocolate-chestnut mixture with the ground almonds. Allow to cool completely before using.

5. Remove the peaches from the marinade with a draining spoon and place them in serving dishes. Fill a pastry bag fitted with a large rosette tube with the chocolate-chestnut mixture.

6. Pipe out a large rosette of chocolate-chestnut mixture into the hollow of each peach half. Place a biscuit on top of each peach and serve chilled, with cream if desired.

Cook's Notes

Time
Peaches take 1 hour to marinate, preparation takes about 40 minutes.

Variations
Nectarine halves may be used instead of peaches.

Preparation
Fresh peaches or nectarines must be placed in the wine and brandy mixture as soon as they are peeled or they will darken.

Serving Ideas
Peach liqueur or brandy may be poured over each peach before filling, if desired.

SERVES 6-8

CASSATA

No sweet selection is complete without ice cream.
The Italian kind is rich, creamy and justly famous.

Almond Layer
2 eggs, separated
½ cup powdered sugar
½ cup heavy cream
½ tsp almond extract

Chocolate Layer
2 eggs, separated
½ cup powdered sugar
½ cup heavy cream
2oz semi-sweet chocolate
2 tbsps cocoa
1½ tbsps water

Fruit Layer
1 cup heavy cream
2 tbsps maraschino or light rum
1 egg white
½ cup powdered sugar
½ cup candied fruit
1oz shelled chopped pistachios

1. To prepare the almond layer, beat egg whites until stiff peaks form, gradually beating in the powdered sugar, a spoonful at a time. Lightly beat the egg yolks and fold in the whites. Whip the cream with the almond extract until soft peaks form, and fold into the egg mixture. Lightly oil an 8 inch round cake pan. Pour in the almond layer mixture and smooth over the top. Cover with plastic wrap and freeze until firm.

2. To prepare the chocolate layer, beat the egg whites until stiff but not dry and gradually beat in the powdered sugar. Whip the cream until soft and fold into the egg white mixture. Put the chocolate in the top of a double boiler over simmering water. Remove it from the heat and stir in the egg yolks. Combine cocoa and water and add to the chocolate mixture. Allow to cool and then fold into the egg white mixture. Spoon the chocolate layer over the almond layer and return, covered, to the freezer.

3. To make the rum fruit layer, whip the cream until soft peaks form. Whip the egg white until about the same consistency as cream. Gradually add the powdered sugar, beating well after each addition. Combine the two mixtures, fold in the rum, fruit and nuts. Spread this mixture on top of the chocolate layer, cover and freeze until firm.

4. To serve, loosen the cassata from around the edges of the pan with a small knife. Place a hot cloth around the pan for a few seconds to help loosen. Turn out onto a serving plate and cut into wedges to serve.

Step 2 Fold the chocolate mixture into the egg white and cream mixture with a rubber spatula or large spoon, taking care not to over fold.

Step 3 Pour the prepared rum fruit layer over the top of the firmly frozen chocolate layer.

Cook's Notes

Time
Preparation can take several hours, so that one ice cream layer can freeze before another is added.

Preparation
Whisk the cream softly; over-whisking will cause it to separate. Whisk the egg whites in between each addition of sugar. If sugar is added too quickly, egg whites will not stiffen sufficiently.

Serving Ideas
Sprinkle the top layer of the cassata with more chopped pistachios and chocolate curls. Decorate with rosettes of whipped cream, if desired. Can be served with a fruit or chocolate sauce or with maraschino poured over the top.

SERVES 6-8

ZUPPA INGLESE

This is Italy's tribute to trifle. The name means
English soup, but the custard is rich and thick.

2 tbsps cornstarch
2 cups milk
2 eggs, lightly beaten
2 tbsps sugar
Grated rind of ½ a lemon
Pinch nutmeg
1 punnet ripe strawberries
16 ladyfingers
Amaretto
½ cup heavy cream

1. Mix the cornstarch with some of the milk. Beat the eggs, sugar lemon rind and nutmeg together and pour in the remaining milk. Mix with the cornstarch mixture in a heavy-based pan and stir over gentle heat until the mixture thickens and comes to the boil.

2. Allow to boil for 1 minute or until the mixture coats the back of a spoon. Place a sheet of wax paper directly on top of the custard and allow it to cool slightly.

3. Save 8 even-sized strawberries for garnish and hull the remaining ones. Place half of the ladyfingers in the bottom of a glass bowl and sprinkle with some of the amaretto. Cut the strawberries in half and place a layer on top of the ladyfingers. Pour a layer of custard on top and repeat with the remaining sliced strawberries and ladyfingers. Top with another layer of custard and allow to cool completely.

4. Whip the cream and spread a thin layer over the top of the set custard. Pipe the remaining cream around the edge of the dish and decorate with the reserved strawberries. Serve chilled.

Step 1 Combine the custard ingredients in a heavy-based saucepan and cook until the mixture thickens and coats the back of a spoon.

Step 3 Place a layer of lady-fingers and strawberries in a serving dish and coat with a layer of custard. Repeat with remaining ingredients.

Step 4 Decorate the top using a pastry bag fitted with a rosette tube.

Cook's Notes

Time
Preparation takes about 20 minutes, custard takes about 5 minutes to cook.

Variations
Decorate the top of the dessert with grated chocolate, toasted almonds or shelled pistachios in addition to, or instead of, the strawberries. Other fruit may be used, if desired.

INDEX

ACKNOWLEDGMENT
The publishers wish to thank the following suppliers
for their kind assistance:
Corning Ltd for providing Pyrex and other cookware.
Habasco International Ltd for the loan of basketware.
Stent (Pottery) Ltd for the loan of glazed pottery oven-
to-table ware.

Compiled by Judith Ferguson
Photographed by Peter Barry
Designed by Philip Clucas and Sara Cooper
Recipes Prepared for Photography by
Jacqueline Bellefontaine